How To Buy The Perfect Gift

By

Georgia Mae Rose

Copyright Scott McDowell 2019

Table of contents

Why does finding a great present matter? 5
Its About Them 7
What reaction? 9
Needs vs wants 12
Prized Possessions 15
Values 17
Goals 20
Dreams 22
Research 24
How Much? 27
Imbalance 30
The Replacement 33
Nostalgia 35
Object or Experience 37
Pleasure or Fulfilment 41
The Opening Experience 43
The Recurring Present 50
Custom gifts 53
Humor 56
A New World 58
Secret Santa is Meh 60

Regifting *64*
Pitching In *68*
Many or One *70*
Children *75*
Life Partners *78*
Older People *81*
The Worst Possible Gifts *85*
Expectation and Comparison *88*
Review *90*
Conclusion *91*

Why does finding a great present matter?

The same reason taking no thought in the words you use matters, some words hurt, some are meaningless and some mean the world to you.

If you want people to like you, treat them well. If you want people to trust you, treat them well consistently.

You can change someone's life with a present, fulfil a dream, help them out of a bad situation or you can show them no thought what so ever and give them another pair of socks. How do you think someone feels when you get them socks year after year? Do you think this person believes you really listen to them and knows who they are? The obvious answer is NO.

If you don't think about someone, do you really care about them? Not a lot, those people get a lot of socks.

Gifts are an opportunity, you should use this opportunity to create bonds, bury grudges, rekindle old relationships and improve existing ties with everyone you reach out to.

If you think of it as just a burden, it will be.

If you think of it as an opportunity, it is.

Creating a shared moment can make all the difference.

"Happiness quite unshared can scarcely be called happiness; it has no taste."

— ***Charlotte Bronte***

Its About Them

It's easy to know what you want, what's hard is knowing what others want.

You have to come to the realization that not everyone thinks like you, they are not in the same situation, not in the same environment, have different needs and wants, some things you understand, some you don't understand and never could.

Some things you might be against morally but really it doesn't matter, because remember *ITS NOT ABOUT YOU!*

Your feelings don't count when it comes to other people's needs and wants. Feelings are not facts, and they are definitely not rational at all times.

When you see something and say that looks good, it doesn't mean your friends will agree, it doesn't mean your wife or husband will like it, it doesn't mean your mum will like it. It just means that you like it and guess what, ITS NOT

ABOUT YOU!

"Compassion may be defined as the capacity to be attentive to the experience of others, to wish the best for others, and to sense what will truly serve others."

— **Joan Halifax**

What reaction?

What reaction do you hope to get, if any?

Hoping to get a reaction is fair, demanding a reaction is crazy behavior.

For the people you love, you want them to be happy.

For the people you just get along with and need it to go without a hitch, you want them to accept it without cause for judgment.

For the people you dislike but still have to buy for, you hope it doesn't even create any mental activity and just goes un-noticed.

Buying peoples affection can only go so far, its not a magic bullet and never will be, the person you are and the way you treat someone can't be totally forgotten just because you bought something shiny and expensive. It might be a very nice band aid for a while but its temporary, it's just buying time.

Treat people well year-round and you will get smiles before the present is opened.

Similarly, the amount of thought you put into finding a present the recipient wants can mean more than the price of the present. The amount of money made and the sweat you had to endure to buy the present doesn't always equate to a better gift, although a little thought a little money and sweat together can make for a great present.

A little boy won't appreciate an Armani suit no matter how good he looks he would rather have an action man a football and a game for his xbox or playstation.

You can try your best to get a massively positive reaction, look to their dreams, fix their problems and end their suffering, but if all you do is put a little smile on their face, that's enough.

"Any fool can criticize, complain, and condemn—and most fools do. But it takes character and self-control to be understanding and forgiving."

– **Dale Carnegie**

Needs vs wants

Should you buy a present that fulfils a need or a want? Maybe

To be sensible or not, that is the question.

Most people are pleasure seeking, instant gratification addicts that buy themselves wants rather than needs year-round. It is the rare person that only buys what they need and very rarely want.

So, what do we do? Give presents that will not be well received to each group to balance out their lives or just give them something they would buy themselves?

I think this touches on the question, do we want to be liked or do we want to help the person in front of us?

If the person in front of you has a reasonably good life, why try to fix them when they are not suffering? They will put themselves together at the pace they choose. I would say fulfilling more wants than needs seem reasonable as the average person will take care of their success over time. I would say it's a judgment call you should not over worry about.

If someone has a life that is falling apart and you can fulfil a need they will never tend to, it can't be a bad thing. They might not smile when they receive the gift, they might even think less of you, but you might help someone out of a hole they can't climb themselves.

The needs versus wants question is a difficult one, a sensible person could do with some fun and a pleasure seeker could do with some help, both might not be happy to change their usual pattern of behavior. All you can do is try your best and that is good enough.

Hopefully your sense will prevail. For a more in depth look into wants and needs you can always look to Maslow's Hierarchy of needs, even though this might be difficult when you are out looking for a gift.

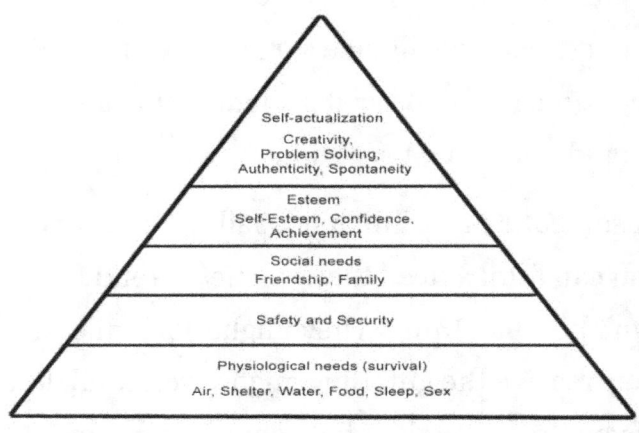

"Supply the needs first and the wants later, for one can only obtain true peace, love and joy when one supplies the needs first and not the wants."

— **David Benedict Zumbo**

Prized Possessions

What are the recipients prized possession or possessions?

This is such a great little cheat for finding a present that someone will at least like, and maybe love.

One of the easiest ways to take advantage of this is to buy an add-on type product or service to compliment the item they love. New mats for the car, toys for the doll's house, flowers for the garden, books for the library.

It's hard to feel mis-understood when someone buys you something that applies to your own favorite things. It shows you take notice of the person and what they are interested in, what they value and feel some connection to.

Maybe the prized possession seems shallow or mundane to us but it doesn't matter, its beside the point of finding something another person would actually care about.

Hopefully the recipient of the gift will realize the fact you noticed them and took account of their passions and interests with this gift.

"There is no possession more valuable than a good and faithful friend."

— **Socrates**

Values

If you know and understand someone's values, it's like looking in the engine or the back of the watch to see what make someone tick.

If you understand what drives a person to do the things they do, in the order they do them you can get along with and help that person in ways no one else can.

We all have different values, for some people this comes as a shock but people are very different when it comes to their value system.

What is a value system, a value system is the funnel which you prioritize, the most important things through It's your personal hierarchy of importance, if family is the most important thing to you, then you will see the world through that lens, if your personal achievements are the most important thing to you the same principle applies.

People have multiple values, for instance a

person's top 5 values could be Family then, Career, friends, food and holidays. If you can kind of get an idea of this person's top values it helps you know when you have found something they will actually like.

Knowing another person's values is the closest we are likely to get to seeing the world through another person's eyes.

How do we find out what our friends or family's values are? We look at where they expel most of their mental and physical energy. Do they constantly send messages and make phone calls to the family, do they arrange meet ups between everyone? Do they spend all their time fixing up their home to make it a special place? Do they spend all their time in the office even though they don't need to? People might not like the fact that the things they do the most are some of, if not the highest value things in their life.

A person's values don't always make sense to other people, some of us have very shallow values but that doesn't mean we should be ashamed of them, we probably inherited most of them, so you might as well just enjoy them.

If you apply this principle you will start seeing things the other person will want on a day to day basis If you have got a lot of time to find a present it will be so much easier now you understand the person you're buying for.

Not everyone is proud of their values, some people love the television, there is nothing wrong with that. Its ok to binge watch a series if you love it, and it's good for the buyer of presents to know about something you love.

I imagine some grandparents who can only sit all day in front of the tv due to illness would love a new television this year.

"It's not hard to make decisions when you know what your values are."

— **Roy Disney**

Goals

Do they have any goals you know about?

What are your friends, family and lovers walking towards?

Can you help them, or make the experience more enjoyable, maybe keep them motivated for a while longer?

A student could do with the books, a reminder of what he's doing it for, something to sit on his desk that makes him smile every time he's buried in paperwork.

A business owner might need a book on something they don't know how to handle, an athlete might need new trainers to remain competitive, a car restorer might be looking for a part that is difficult to find.

Whatever you can do to make their journey towards their goal easier, more enjoyable or even possible is a great present. Even if it's boring to you.

If their journey towards the goal is a ten-step process and you make 1 step manageable, I think it's a job well done.

Imagine how much further along people would be if someone helped them on their path. You can be that person who came out of nowhere and made it happen for someone.

"Setting goals is the first step in turning the invisible into the visible."

— **Tony Robbins**

Dreams

A vision for your life or a one-off event you always wanted to experience.

Do you know the recipient's dreams? If you have known someone a long time you probably do know them and if you don't it's a great conversation to have.

Where would you live? What would you do day to day? Where would you travel too? Would you work? Own a business? Run a charity? Join a cause like the U.N. peace corps? Spend your time surfing? You will probably learn more in this conversation than you have in the last 10 years together.

If you can extract their dreams for their life you might be able to fulfil something amazing for them, or a small part of it.

You could write them a plan to get their dream, make it into baby steps and buy the recipient the first step to go with the plan.

Maybe you could get the whole family to chip in towards the dream, maybe it will take more than one year to build up this dream present, but that's still a lot better than a pair of socks.

2 years' worth of air miles built up over Christmas and birthdays to pay for that dream trip, 2 years' worth of classes.

Whatever it may be or whatever it takes, this endeavor is a virtuous one.

What more can you do than try to make a dream come true.

"If one advances confidently in the direction of his dreams, and endeavors to live the life which he has imagined, he will meet with a success unexpected in common hours."

—Henry David Thoreau

Research

Your main recipients of your gifts are you new research project, and how much you know about them will help determine how well your present is received.

Obviously, you don't want to invade their privacy like a tech company looking through their internet history or a stalker going through their wardrobe. Reasonable noble detective work for the reasonable noble purpose of giving them something nice.

Start with the obvious and ask them what they want? That doesn't sound like your usual research project but it gets straight to the point. If you get a list of presents, you are off to a great start and you can think about the list and see if you can find something even better than they ask for.

Some people are too shy to ask for what they want.

If you don't get a list, we start thinking about all the things we know they are interested in. You can make a little list. Then you can make a list of things they used to do years ago. A list of places and things they would like to experience or have enjoyed previously. Hopefully you are getting a sense of who they are now.

Do they have any skills or talents, what did they do for work, did they work on anything outside their jobs, were they involved with the military or a charity?

What do they do on a daily basis, do they have a gym, work, classes, home to family routine or something else you can think of?

You can google your friends and look through their Facebook, LinkedIn profiles to find out things you don't know. This might be a bit on the spying end of the continuum but it's for a good cause, if you get caught doing this you might come off as being creepy, so be careful with this reconnaissance mission, not everyone will come away with no scars.

You can try asking other members of the family/social circle what they would be interested in right now. This can be a great for finding out things they don't talk to you about because they think you will not be interested or just haven't brought it up in conversation recently.

Try to find out their plans for the new year when you chat, where are they going, holidays etc. Are they going to their gym membership or their other classes? You can help them stay motivated and excited for all these things with new equipment or information on the subject.

The more you learn the more you earn is a common saying in business circles, maybe this statement applies to giving gifts to your love one, but instead of earning your laughing and smiling.

"Give me six hours to chop down a tree and I will spend the first four sharpening the axe."

— **Abraham Lincoln**

How Much?

How much is enough? How much is too much?

The price? The amount of effort displayed? The number of presents?

Welcome to the awkwardness that is unequal gifting, it happens to all of us, it is almost impossible to avoid, even if you arrange to spend the same amount on each other, as no one can stick to a plan 100% of the time.

It is good to remind yourself this will happen to you, so don't feel flustered when someone gifts you something of ten times the value you give to them. Accept the present with grace appreciate it for what it is and don't fall into the trap of comparison.

If you are in a relationship, you could discuss the amount spent to avoid any negative reaction. You don't want to fall short or over deliver to the point your partner has a leash around your neck. Some people look at the presents and try to figure out what the present is trying to say, what is the meaning behind the present? Mostly there will be no meaning behind the present, the act of giving gifts is the show of appreciation or gratitude for another person. And that is enough.

Some people will want to see you have gone to some expense within your means, which displays a small sacrifice to them, some want to see you have made an effort whether it being in thoughtfulness, time or sweat. Some people hope for multiple presents to exchange from someone close to them which adds to the experience.

Some of these things seem unreasonable to expect, even a little bit crazy on the part of the recipient. These expectations have been manifested through observations of the giver and the recipient's previous life experiences.

You need to become pro-active when it comes to the giving and receiving of presents, especially where emotions are high. If the present could make or break a relationship that is fragile or create animosity between everyone, you need to set the stage, create rules for gifting, enough of a present to be grateful but not beyond the budget that might hurt the family budget etc.

Make your own rules based on your own unique circumstances and make sure to stick to the pact.

Breaking the pact could lead to mis-trust, so don't betray your agreement no matter how well intentioned you are.

"The excellence of a gift lies in its appropriate - ness rather than in its value."

-Charles Dudley Warner

Imbalance

Don't worry about the imbalance

The chance of there being no imbalance in gift value are very slim. The only way to stop this happening is by working it before hand and agreeing to a set price, number of items etc.

If you don't make a plan together there is always going to be an imbalance, so ready yourself for this, accept it as if it has already happened for better and for worse.

Prime your mind for what is coming. Let's go through the experience.

If you buy more things, pay more money and make more effort its ok, you should not care or mention it.

If you do the opposite, its ok not to care or mention it as well.

The worst thing you can do is bring it up, giving attention to the imbalance, giving attention to the fact someone did too little or too much. It's easier to just accept the gesture and be grateful.

In the previous chapter we talked about how you can avoid this by creating an agreement, in this chapter we will talk about when it all goes wrong and the imbalances are just too obvious to ignore for your emotionally charged exchange.

Always keep the receipt!

Offer to get the refund and take the person to a nice place to find something more appropriate and probably more expensive. Buy lunch and let them know you tried your best the first-time round.

If you bought your wife a pair of socks and she bought you a car, offer to spend some money on seeing a psychiatrist about your money issues.

If your wife buys you a car the family can't afford don't offer her counselling as a present, but take back the car. Life is not fair is it.

Make up for your lack of a decent present with an offer of disproportionate value in the future, like picking out a holiday etc.

If someone buys a present which puts the family or individual in debt, do not immediately react negatively, enjoy your day and get the receipt go the present giver in a couple of days. Say that you appreciate the gift but we can't afford it or it's not necessary to put yourself into debt for.

These things happen from time to time, they are best avoided, but they are no reason to lose family and friends over. Some people make a mountain out of a mole hill in all sorts of situations, this is just another event where the creation of unnecessary drama could unfold.

Be forgiving to the people who make mistakes. You have to remind yourself that you have made mistakes over this lifetime which makes you one in the same.

"It is said that gifts persuade even the gods."

— **Euripides**

The Replacement

Replace a lost item.

The story of a terrible loss, a dream given up, an item that had been stolen or misplaced. All the ways we can lose in life and in time.

What has your friend or family lost along the span of their life, even the time you have known each other. Have they been a victim of theft, a mugging, did they lose something in an accident or giveaway a prized possession in the divorce?

How they lost the item might not be what we should focus on, can you replace the item that was taken and bring back some dignity and restore their pride. This could be a turning point for the person who had a major loss in life, and this symbol of pulling things back together might make a difference. It's worth a try no matter the result.

Helping someone back from a bad patch is a noble thing to do. And this gesture might be the thing that gets them out of depression and picks up their spirit so they can fight on with life's day to day struggles.

You can be a heroic part of the story, an inspiration when times are tough. A replacement gift is a good start to help out.

"There's always failure. And there's always disappointment. And there's always loss. But the secret is learning from the loss, and realizing that none of those holes are vacuums."

— **Michael J. Fox**

Nostalgia

Shared memories, and moments of triumph in their life

Great memories shared or just revered, sports, movies and hobbies of days past. Likely given up for the practicality of a good living, a pay cheque and the safety and security of chasing money to keep a roof over your loved ones.

It's a good choice a noble choice but we still like to remember the person we used to be, the many previous variations of yourself and the moments that made it special.

How can we take advantage of this?

By giving them a taste of their youth, a day out doing what they used to love paid for by you, a symbol of those times maybe a sport shirt with their name and number on the back or something of similar effect. A retro games console you used to play together with the games you used to play, a book they always read as a child. Whatever you understand to be a great moment in their life, you can symbolize with a gift.

"Symbols are the imaginative signposts of life."

— **Margot Asquith**

Object or Experience

Should you buy someone a gift they can feel and touch or give them a voucher for an experience to enjoy?

Happiness is usually increased by experiences more than objects, but the problem with an experience as a present is? You can't experience it when you receive it, you can't touch it or feel like you will feel when you get there.

Experiences usually just look like a credit card with writing on top when you give it out.

How to give an experience present with the X factor of an object.

Get a big box, add small experience related materials to the box with the voucher waiting at the bottom of the box. For example, you could have a hiking voucher hidden by hiking magazines and a flash light.

You can get as creative as you possibly want with this, so go crazy. Put a ticket to Disney inside a bunch of flowers or at the bottom of a birthday cake. Be careful not to cut the tickets to pieces.

Sometimes an experience is not the best present for someone, if the recipient has agoraphobia and has panic attacks in public places or if the person is just too busy to take time away from work and family, everyone is different and has a different situation to contend with.

If someone wants a certain object then go with the object, why fight someone else's motivations.

Experiences do beat objects for happiness in all the studies, but sometimes it's just not practical or as easy to pick out a winning experience every time. The day they go to the experience it will probably rain and they will have an argument on the way, you can't control the way they will feel on the day or how the experience will be on the day.

The thing is, people will not be looking back on the things they had in their lives as much as the experiences they had. People always wish they had more experiences in their lives and no amount of stuff can ever make up for that.

Work out what the person loves and notice how they react in different environments. You can see the emotion on someone's face when they are in a place they like or they talk about it, any clue is better than none. Maybe you can bring up the experience without talking about presents. Have you ever been white water rafting, I always wanted to do that? Let them answer and give you some ideas about a present.

Between objects and experiences type gifts are objects made for experiences, like a skate board, kite, bike, guitar, catcher's mitt and any other object that requires you to try some type of activity. This present could be collecting dust for the next year or become a new obsession, a passion that lights up someone's life for decades to come.

If you can buy an experience and an object for

someone you have covered both bases, you can't lose.

"Whatever money I made, I did not buy an apartment or a car: I bought plane tickets and hotels and experiences."

— **Shenaz Treasury**

Pleasure or Fulfilment

Pleasure or fulfilment in a gift.

Both is the best but one is better than none.

Some people go for pleasure and some for fulfilment.

It's the difference between a cooked meal and a cooking class, maybe you like the idea of both. The meal is a temporary pleasure for a few hours to look forward to, the class will teach you how to cook for yourself, take pride in your new skills and make each meal for the rest of your life a little bit better, the classes could even lead to a new career or hobby.

The recipient will probably not see it this way, and most people would rather have some instant gratification from the night at a restaurant relaxing.

I suppose the question this raises is, do you want someone to like you more than, you want a better life for them?

It's not your job to make the recipients life better in the future, unless they are your children that you are helping succeed later in life.

The job of the gift giver is to put a smile on the recipient's face, nothing else.

"Do not bite at the bait of pleasure, till you know there is no hook beneath it"

> **— Thomas Jefferson**

The Opening Experience

Even if you can't find a present that makes a lasting memory, you can make the experience of opening the present something to remember and if you make the opening experience annoying, it will be something to forget. This can add to the novelty and excitement of the event without costing you a small fortune.

The first thing I think of when talking about creative opening experiences is the box inside a box, inside a box where the real present is. It's a fun little thing to do, that is very easy and quick to create. Make sure not to start with a massive present then make them open 6 boxes just to get a pack of underwear, after ten minutes unwrapping. This is the opposite of the effect we want to have, in this scenario the recipient was over joyed with the big present then had his expectations destroyed and ultimately leading to disappointment. We want to have the opposite effect, we want the person to have a high-quality present in the smallest box, an extreme example would be a human size box with a lot of boxes going all the way down to a tiny box with a diamond ring inside. Expectations exceeded rather than destroyed is always the way to go.

You could do the same thing with Russian dolls or something else interesting you can think of.

At Easter you could arrange an egg hunt in the garden, put small amounts of money in plastic eggs and chocolate eggs hidden all over the garden for the children and probably some of the adults to make a mad dash for.

Similar to the Easter egg hunt, but at a more sophisticated level is the scavenger hunt, for the final present at Christmas which happens to be competitive. You can make this as intellectually stimulating, silly, physically demanding, funny and scary as you like. Decode puzzles, race to the next clue, use the compass, dig the hole in the garden and work out the password to open the treasure chest only to find inside, a pair of

Christmas socks, or maybe something a little bit better.

You can go crazy with this and make something up you think everyone would love. For the adults you could leave a note put together from magazine clipping like a serial killer would, leave an old phone on the table, then call the phone with a voice changer so it sounds creepy, "I have the presents held hostage, I will release one present if you perform the needed tasks, if you fail to complete these tasks I will, let's say take care of the presents myself" hahaha click, a timer starts in the background with 60 minutes left and the instructions underneath. Maybe this version could be kept just for the adults who are into mystery murder weekends and tv thrillers. Don't scare the children.

You can use book clues, puzzles that you had specially made for them to put together with a riddle on it. Whatever you can think of that is interesting. A key hidden in the cake (make sure no one swallows it, if you do put it inside a plastic capsule like a tiny Tupperware. You could even put one of you lists of instructions or clues inside balloons you blew up sitting around the room you have been in all day.

Aside from the scavenger hunts there are all the old classics like putting a bow around a car or the new family pet's jumper.

You can make all sorts of games for everyone to participate in for presents. Why not make your board games prize orientated, multiple prizes for all the winners, Monopoly, Pictionary, Jenga, Scrabble and all the other classics get a little more interesting when there are prizes for winning.

Be careful not to create too many tears with the younger children who have not learned to lose well.

You can create a Christmas wheel of fortune, make a game of who wants to be a millionaire Christmas edition with call a friend in the room. Make a team quiz for the prized bag of gifts.

Play children's party classics like musical chairs,

hot potato, spin the bottle, and rock, paper, scissors with the adults included for a competitive fun way to hive an extra gift.

You could introduce a big family present like a holiday with the help of a video or slideshow you have made then handout the tickets afterwards. Using video and slideshows can be like the trailer to a movie you want to see and add to the anticipation.

A nice way to add an element of surprise, to giving the present is leaving it in places that will shock your recipient in a nice way. You can put a small present in their shoe, their bathroom drawer and shoe cupboard. The oven could be a good one or the microwave, they would have to be bid and obvious enough so you don't leave anything inside and cause a fire. The dishwasher might be good, or the washing machine or dryer, again make sure these are safe and obvious to see. Fridges and freezers will be good for presents they can't damage, maybe put them in a Tupperware box first. If you can leave something in their car, work desk, for a present they will see when you're not around, that would be nice.

You can leave gifts inside other gifts for a clever surprise as well, be sure to make them look inside the present, otherwise they might never see it and it sits there for years never to be used. You can do things like put cinema tickets inside a book, that's inside a jewelry box that's inside a laptop bag, that's inside a suitcase. Let your imagination do its worst with this surprising method of giving gifts.

You can shape presents to look like totally different things while in the packaging, you can even place the present in to boxes and other items to totally trick your recipient.

Timing your gifts can give them a little extra punch. There is definitely something about something good happening unexpectedly that makes it worth remembering. Unusually timed gifts do make for some nice moments, a gift given after they think it's over later in the day.

The day before a Christmas or while driving home for Christmas you give a present to the passenger.

I hope you see how there is almost always a way to make the giving process a little more special if you have the time to get creative and put some thought into it.

Creativity involves breaking out of established patterns in order to look at things in a different way.

   -**Edward De Bono**

The Recurring Present

The gifts that keep on giving.

Why not buy someone a gift they open all year round rather than just the once. One of the best things to make your life better is creating things to look forward to, why not try doing this for someone else.

This could be a digital membership, a physical product or product in a subscription box a lease for something, maybe there is another recurring gift type you can think of that I have missed. There are lots of different recurring products to choose from that will enhance your gift giving powers.

My favorite membership gift is the monthly magazine as its fairly cheap and it caters to every hobby or interest on the planet.

You can get monthly subscriptions of almost everything sent to your door, the list below has some of the most popular subscriptions available as of 2019.

Meal delivery, Books, beauty, golf, fitness, pets, health food, health products, tea, coffee, chocolate, luxury socks, clothing, newspapers, magazines, fishing, vinyl records, wine, cheese, craft beer, camping, hiking, survival, arts and crafts.

You could purchase a more traditional subscription style gift such as a mobile phone contract, pay for streaming services for tv, music and games. Some game consoles can be purchased like a phone contract now.

Monthly entertainment packages like cinema theatre concerts events and so on have monthly and yearly subscriptions. A season ticket for sporting events would be a dream gift for some people.

If you have the budget you could pay for a meal plan or lease a car for them for the year.

Some subscriptions can last for only 3 months, so the cost of certain presents does not mount up to as much as first thought, most subscription offer at least a 6- and 12-month contract to choose from.

Whatever you choose to do, a recurring gift can be a nice thing to give someone.

"Happiness is pretty simple: someone to love, something to do, something to look forward to."

— **Rita Mae Brown**

Custom gifts

The gift that took a little more effort to be a little more personal.

You can buy someone a watch that's great, but buying the watch with a message engraved inside is brilliant. Maybe it's an inside joke you will get engraved, a date that means something to you, a message to keep their spirits up or just to say, I love you. Getting the watch engraved makes it much more than just a watch.

Imagine a watch from a widowed father giving a watch to his son engraved, your mother would be proud of you. The impact your words can have on people just by being added to a physical item is larger than what it should be logically. Luckily were not dealing with the logical were dealing with the emotional and that's the same way with most personalized gifts.

You can also use images to personalize things and show off that moment you captured on pretty much anything you can think of these days, its' not just a t-shirt now it's everything.

You can even get hand and foot prints attached to your gifts.

Get creative with this and make your own unique present that only you could imagine. Make something that would only mean something to you and the recipient.

You could make an anniversary present with an image of the day you met imprinted onto a newspaper or a family crest shield, you could have the date printed on the vase containing flowers and the box of chocolates.

You can make your own cards with your own words and images; this is good if you can't find something appropriate for the occasion or your unique relationship with this person. Your speaking for yourself in this type of card, using your own language and shared humor which makes it more relevant than a card written for the masses.

You can get personalized hammers, dog bowls,

golf balls even heritage plaques commemorating the living person in this household. If you can think of it you can probably get someone to make it these days.

With a little bit of effort and brain power you can create something that will be cherished for years to come. This is a massive winner with the more emotional and sentimental receivers of gifts.

"A thoughtful cup of tea brought to your bedside each morning means more to me than the huge bouquet of flowers bought once a year."

- **Penny Jordan**

Humor

If you're looking at a present which you feel is humorous make sure to consider whether the person you are buying for actually has a sense of humor.

It's hard to believe when you have a sense of humor, that people can live their whole lives without one, but they do.

Some people are to insecure and fragile at certain times in their life they can't take a joke at their expense. When you are young, you can often mistake a joke for a personal attack on your character rather than just a joke. We can take ourselves too seriously because we are trying to hold ourselves up to a certain image or identity that is unsustainable when we are young.

So be careful giving joke presents to the young, the insecure or fragile individual, even the person who might not grasp the joke right away and take it seriously.

"A person without a sense of humor is like a wagon without springs. It's jolted by every pebble on the road."

— **Henry Ward Beecher**

A New World

Open up a new world to someone with an unexpected present outside of their usual territory.

This is a nice thing to do, but it can be hit and miss.

Only try this if you know the person well and have an inkling based on the other interests they enjoy.

For example, it wouldn't be surprising if an ice skater would like roller blading or a snowboarder moving to the beach would like to try surfing. These 2 examples are so closely related it's almost impossible to miss the target, obviously you will encounter more difficult versions of this gift puzzle.

What do you get a person who loves computer games, but you're sick of buying them the same present? Maybe a board game or another competitive type of activity, would they try a competitive sport or try playing low stakes poker?

Getting someone their first telescope, business book (Think and Grow Rich comes to mind), tennis racket, ice skates, set of weights, surf board, spice rack, anything they have yet to explore, is an exciting idea and maybe something you can enjoy together.

If they have mentioned being interested in your hobby maybe you can get them started in this as well. This might help strengthen your relationship and give you both something to talk about.

Expanding someone's horizons can be amazing, it's like your giving birth to a part of someone they have never seen before.

"The most beautiful thing we can experience is the mysterious. It is the source of all true art and science."

— **Albert Einstein**

Secret Santa is Meh

Why do you really want to do secret Santa?

What is it?

What is the alternative to this rubbish?

How you really feel watching the secret Santa show unfold. Good idea for office or work colleagues, maybe. Not so great for the family.

The idea is simply to create an anonymous gift giver. You all put your names into a hat and pick out a name, the name you pick out is the person you will send the gift to anonymously.

You should all stick to a set budget for this, so know crazy colleagues get jealous or feel insecure about the present they purchased.

Some people adapt secret Santa and do it their own way, often picking one name out for everyone to chip in on a present. Leaving the purchase up to someone elected, or arguing over what to buy amongst the group. This also leaves a bunch of losers watching the winner open something while you keep a happy face on, it's a little bit like watching the reactions of people who came runner up at the Oscars.

Why do we do this to ourselves people, what fresh tinsel covered hell is this, I have to buy a present for the random person I held the elevator for once this year, why did I buy him a wash kit including shower gel and deodorant, is he going to take it the wrong way, I have never smelled the guy. I hope he never finds out I was his secret Santa.

What is so good about being an anonymous giver? If this was really such a good idea gift tags would have died out years ago. Would you want a Christmas where the family just put random presents in the middle of the floor and everyone got a plain package with no identity attached?

What did you get Tommy Junior? A Cinderella costume and a packet of cigarettes, thanks everyone. What did you get Sally Junior? A screw driver set and a classic cars monthly magazine. What did Dad get? A pair of socks and a size 2 pair of roller blades, Merry Christmas.

Why gifting should rarely be anonymous. You give a gift to try make the receivers life a little brighter, to say I notice you and what your about, I see what makes you an individual and I'm trying to honor that with a gift.

The best gifts are never anonymous.

Even a raffle is better for all the cash that gets put in. At least everyone gets to participate in the occasion.

The best thing to do is probably go old school, send everyone a card or an email saying merry Christmas and buy a present for someone you are grateful to have in your life, it's probably best to do this without the whole office knowing. The receiver might feel like they have to buy you a present now and resent you for it, but it's unlikely and the gift will be appreciated.

"The main reason Santa is so jolly is because he knows where all the bad girls live."

— **George Carlin**

Regifting

Regifting, giving a present you received to another person.

Be careful if you decide to do this. Think before you stink.

Never regift if you have forgotten who actually gave you the present. Just sell the item and use the money to buy something that will not cause you trouble.

Never regift to someone who shares the same social circle or social media, again its more trouble than it's worth.

Check the item for writing, don't leave a gift tag on the item, look in the front pages of book to see if someone has written something. If it's a gift card, check to see there is money still on there, if the number is odd 17.17 the recipient will guess that it was regifted.

If regifting is your only option, maybe you could find a way to make the item look new or just different. If you were gifting a phone, you could restore it to factory settings and put a new case on it, still without the box and packaging it's still fairly obvious it's a regift. You could paint a bike or change the cover of a seat cushion on a chair.

If you can do something to make your gift look like it was your idea and you were not simply passing it on, why not give it a try.

"Why do 'slow down' and 'slow up' mean the same thing? Why is the third hand on the watch called the second hand?" — **George Carlin**

Shared Gifts

What are shared gifts?

You buy a ticket to an experience or an event to go with your friend or partner. You buy something that you can both enjoy like a board game, poker table, golf clubs, cinema tickets, whatever it is you both would actually enjoy doing together.

I imagine some people are thinking don't make this popular, I will have to attend all these days out I don't really want to participate in. I recommend giving these gifts to people that actually enjoy your company, anything else is pushing your luck.

For someone who is lonely or just left to themselves too often, this could be the best gift they get. The surprise of someone they care about wanting to spend time with them for once, might be a bigger gift than you can imagine.

How much of our family and friends are neglected and left alone most of the year? This has increased due to the digital age and the lack of necessity to actually see each other.

Like most things the digital age is a gift and a curse. The comforts of the digital age can detract from the camaraderie we feel, and before everything was on demand, delivered to the door, instantly mailed, answered by a search engine we had to look into another person's eyes and see our shared experience.

There is no going back, and life is getting better. Don't forget to share a little time with someone, so it makes all this progress worth it.

"There is real value in sharing moments that don't live forever."

— **Evan Spiegel**

Pitching In

Pitching in for presents is a great way to ensure a higher quality present, maybe even a life changing one.

You could all chip in to fix a problem with their car, pay towards medical care that they have been putting off, help pay off their credit card debt, pay for a course to help them switch careers.

Maybe you could pay for your Mum to have her house cleaned once a week for a year with your siblings.

If you can't afford a present that is very good, pitching in with family or friends for something better is likely to be a great option. Avoid arguments about the gift and try to make sure the recipients needs and wants are kept in the minds of everyone.

Pitch in to buy air miles to give a travel gift, holiday, air miles, accommodation etc.

Pitching in together opens up so many different options which were just off the table when you could only use a small sum of money. Your also more likely to encounter discounts on larger orders.

Will pitching in solve your gift buying problems? Possibly

Unity is strength... when there is teamwork and collaboration, wonderful things can be achieved.

— **Mattie Stepanek**

Many or One

Multiple gifts or a few or one gift, that is the question.

What is the answer? It depends!

Unfortunately, like much of life, the devil is in the details.

If you can pull off a guaranteed win with the one larger present that is highly desired by the person receiving the gift, you should go for it.

If you can't be sure to please the person with the larger gift, why not spread the risk with multiple presents, one of the good things about this option is that the time opening gifts last a little longer.

If you go over the top and buy loads of small worthless presents, you have gone too far and ruined the experience. Always try to keep a good balance of quality versus quality in every area of your life.

You get to hedge your bets with multiple presents if you don't want to take the risk on one.

You might not get the big reaction you were hoping for with the big gift, but you will get multiple chances to get a smile on their face.

"When I take a risk, I like it to be a calculated risk, meaning I make it as small as possible."

— **David Green**

Baby Gifts

A new hope, another life, our hopes and dreams, welcome to the world, you are our future.

You also grow too fast for us to keep up, change so fast that we make mistakes and between the family make loads of purchases that never get used.

Making the best of communicating with the family is key to not wasting this opportunity. You can receive 10 times the amount of clothes needed for year 1 or you can communicate and have 4 years of clothes ready. You can do this every year; you don't need 10 years of 2-year old's clothes and 10 years of 3-year-old clothes the next year.

This is an extreme example, but it makes sense if your short of funds, make sure to speak to everyone.

This works for toy age ranges, clothes and

anything else you can think of. A years' worth of nappy vouchers would probably be a well-received gift, not the most glamorous present but a well needed one.

Everyone wants to buy the trainers for the baby because they are cute, but you don't want 25 pairs of baby trainers, they will be the wrong size in 25 weeks.

How well the presents are received will not be dictated by the baby, but the parents who are probably tired, cranky and looking for some help about now.

Always ask what they need for now and next year, what would make their life easier if they had it for the baby.

Your dealing with the parent's values. If the parents are teachers, I'm guessing education would be one of the highest values in their lives. Education toys will probably be appreciated more so than other random gifts. If your gift matches the values of the parents you have made a decent effort.

Still ask what they need and want.

Parents, communicate with your family and friends and get your calendar out to work out how much stuff you need and when you will need it.

There will always be waste, but less is wasted presents is a good aim to have.

I knew I was an unwanted baby when I saw that my bath toys were a toaster and a radio.

— **Joan Rivers**

Children

The answer is they have a list of things they want, and if they don't have one, they will write you one. If they are not allowed to write one, they will have some ideas in their head.

Make sure its age appropriate in the eyes of the parents and in the eyes of the child. They grow out of things at an alarming rate and last year's cool is this year's embarrassing childish present.

I don't think there are many children in the western world writing Christmas lists full of needs, and practical things. They are looking to have fun at all times, wants, wants, wants, play, create, laugh and run, they sound very sane in comparison to the buttoned-up adults hoping for a new clean shirt or a pair of shoes. What happened to us all?

Try to remember the children of your childhood, what you wanted as a child might be 30 years out of date, and a broken version of what is available today. Would you want the brick mobile phone from the 80's? Your dad had one, are you sure you don't want it? A phone is just a phone, right? No. Some things come back in fashion or their brands are revitalized but that's a 1 in a thousand, unfortunately most thing go to the out of date graveyard, never to appear again.

Every generation is different, every child is different, so try to find out what they like, want, think is interesting just like you would with an adult.

They are probably a little bit more advanced than previous generations as well. When your born into a world where you ask google why rather than your parents it's not surprising.

Your junior encyclopedia can't compete with the internet, today's children just know more.

You still have some adult responsibility to help your child find things and experience things outside of their bedroom and their game console.

Some parents have wrapped their children up in so much cotton wool that it's no surprise they have become better at entertaining themselves indoors. They haven't built up the repertoire of games and face to face social skills to play outside.

The original first-person shooter games were kids with water pistols and potato guns running around the streets, another problem for the children is having very few friends that want to play outside now, it's not as much fun playing outside with just 2 people.

Hopefully you can give them what they want, inspire them to try new things and expand their horizons, just like you would for an adult you cared about.

"A person's a person, no matter how small."

— **Dr. Seuss**

Life Partners

For people who find it hard to say, I love and care about you and never had it growing up. Giving gifts might have been a way of communicating their affection.

For the people who show their feelings through words this could be missed. You could mistake a gift to be just a gift, rather than an expression of someone's feelings of gratitude for you.

You can see why gifts are more important when it comes to life partners. You can't afford to be seen making no effort, well not if you want a good relationship.

If your trying to build a life together, why not buy something that contributes towards that shared dream. If your partner talks about moving somewhere far away you want to live, why not plan a weekend in a hotel near there and go and look at the neighborhoods'.

What can you do to make the other persons

quality of life better? An upgrade on the car lease? A new laptop that doesn't crash while they are trying to work? What else have they been putting off, that they really need?

Most partners will tell you what they want, so ask. You will probably end up with a list as long as your arm to pick from. A good question to ask now is which 1 or 2 presents matter the most?

If you can't get a list and they don't need anything and there are no shared dreams it's all about the wants!

In previous chapters we have talked about how to find peoples values, look at their goals and trying to take note of who they are and what they are interested in now. This is your research project, they are your research project, what makes them tick, laugh, listen closely, love to talk about or has some special meaning to them.

Find out what they really like, not what you hoped they would like and follow through on providing those things.

If your partner buys you terrible presents every

year, chuck this book at them.

"Don't try to convince your partner you are right. Instead of trying to win arguments, try to have a winning relationship."

— **Karen Salmansohn**

Older People

What do old people want?

Well the first thing to realize about old people is they are people; they didn't just drop in on the planet from there time machine. They have watched more tv shows, movies, read more books and had more hobbies than you have even tried.

And don't think that just because someone has got more years on the clock than you, they don't have dreams like you, and things they would like to do and see.

Don't think that older people don't want to experience the wonders of the present day. I'm sure grandad would love a 4k tv and would even try watching avatar in 3d, why wouldn't he. If your grandmother loves books, maybe an E-Reader loaded with thousands of books would be a nice present, especially if the book case is overloaded with paperbacks, or for use when travelling.

What does everyone buy old people? Old movies, old music, old books, old everything.

Do you realize that old people are living through all the generations that you are?

They heard all the music come out in the last 10 years and hated or loved it just as much as anyone else. They probably watched Downton Abbey and Game of Thrones, so why are you buying Grandad the Monty Python collection and a Buddy Holly CD?

Some people just stop living at an age they think is old, that is true. But some don't because they are still sane, it's insane to think I'm going to sit and do nothing until the day I die, because now I think I'm old.

Some people think they are old at 50 and settle in to sitting and doing nothing, they are healthy with no injuries but the lines starting to come through on their face has got them tricked into a retirement from living.

If your 50 and live until your over a hundred which is very possible these days, you're not even middle aged, you have only had your independence say 30 years, you have got another 50 plus years of independent living to go. Even if you're a healthy-ish 80 you could have another 30 years of getting busy living.

The oldest person in history lived until 124, there have been some unverified people claiming to live until 150, if the 80-year-old just lived to the verified age of the oldest person at 124 they would have 44 years to live. When you consider some people act old at 50, and you might live 44 years after your 80th birthday, it makes you realize what a delusional way to live it is.

Why do I bring this up? So, you can help stop this from happening in your family. With your attitude towards the older generations improving and the way you interact and approach conversations with older people evolving.

It can all start with the gifts you give to the older people in your family or social circle, reflecting who they are and not just their date of birth.

Maybe you can inspire them to keep going or get going, open a new world up to them from the new generation or re-ignite one of their old passions that fell by the way side.

Grandma Moses started painting at 78, her paintings sell for millions these days, Harry Bernstein wrote The Invisible Wall at 96, Colonel Sanders started KFC at 62 and Ray Kroc bought his first McDonalds at 59 so it's not over until you say it's over, or your health fails you. I hope you carry this sentiment throughout your long life.

I hope your present lights a fire in the heart of someone.

Don't just give them a present, give them a passion, interest, hobby, something to dream about and become excited about all year round.

"Age is an issue of mind over matter. If you don't mind, it doesn't matter." — **Mark Twain**

The Worst Possible Gifts

The gift for you, not the recipient.

The worst type of examples I can think of are the husband buying his wife a really great vacuum cleaner so she can clean the house or the wife buying her husband power tools for the job he has explained he does not want to do.

It can still get worse.

The bad memory trigger symbol, an example of this could buying someone a frame with a picture of all your old friends which included their ex-partner. That is a memory they might not want to go back to much, it definitely won't be getting hanged on the wall, especially if the new partner has something to do with it. Another example would be buying camouflage clothing for an ex-army veteran who suffers from post-traumatic stress.

An easier trap to fall in is the next one.

Do you even know who I am? The question you

don't want to get from your significant other when you buy something that would not interest them in the slightest. If you don't want this to happen, you better do your research, start listening more and try to stop thinking of everything from your perspective.

The overly practical gift for the depressed person waiting for some joy at Christmas is another mistake. What does overly practical mean, I would say its buying someone something they need rather than want, something with no emotional impact that will not even illicit a fake smile at Christmas. If someone is just getting through a divorce, give them something uplifting like a day out rather than a box of legal pads, pens and other stationery.

If it has been a particularly tough year for the family and you can afford to be a little less practical, go for it and put a smile on someone's face.

We can all make mistakes when giving gift, so

don't be too hard on yourself if you make one now and then, it happens to us all.

"The excellence of a gift lies in its appropriateness rather than in its value."

— **Charles Dudley Warner**

Expectation and Comparison

Expectation and Comparison are the thieves of joy.

They can lead to jealousy and a false sense of entitlement, neither of them being based on reality.

If this is true, what would be the giver of joy? Gratitude.

The choice to be grateful makes all the difference, you can look for the positive or negative in anything, even when there is no need to be the judge.

You get what your given and can't change it in the moment, so appreciate the effort another human being has made, to make you happy.

You can't magically get the reaction you wanted either, so learn to appreciate the smallest amount of positivity from your recipients.

As long as the person receiving the gift doesn't

try to hit you over the head with your gift don't make too much of it.

It can feel awkward when receiving a present with people watching, hoping for you to be overcome with joy. So, take that into account when watching other people open presents and thank you for the gift.

You can't always get what you want, you can't always get others what they want, things are rarely equal or fair.

But this is how the cards have fallen so you might as well enjoy the moment, the Stoic philosophy known as Amor Fati (love fate) is appropriate, you accept and look for the things you love in this current reality, as its all you have got.

If all you have got is a pair of Christmas socks, you might as well enjoy them.

"God, grant me the serenity to accept the things I cannot change, The Courage to change the things I can, and wisdom to know the difference."   — **Reinhold Niebuhr**

Review

Please feel free to leave an honest review at - Amazon/

Reviews can make all the difference when trying to get people to read your books. Your feedback is always appreciated and I'm grateful that you picked up this book.

Thank You.

Keep reading for the conclusion and the cheat sheet.

Conclusion

What is our conclusion to your gift giving conundrum?

Get out of your own head and into the person who will be receiving the gifts mind the best you can, think about their hobbies, childhood, teenage years, sports, jobs, places they loved and lived in, their favorite music, movies, sports heroes, historic characters, and things they are just curious and interested in.

Imagine walking in their shoes as much as you can, what are their hopes and dreams for the future, what problems are they facing that you can help them avoid, what can you treat them to that they would never treat themselves to.

Communicate to the best of your ability with all the people you really want to please with your presents. Ask what they want, make a plan to spend similar or the same amounts on each other, get a Christmas list with priority presents at the top and talk about the things you like.

What is guaranteed to put a smile on this person's face?

The quality of answers we get, will be dictated by the quality of the questions we ask ourselves. Which questions have we covered or not covered, that relate to your recipient the most?

If you save yourself from one gifting blunder or improve one relationship even for the shortest time, my job has been done. I hope you got more than just some ideas for presents out of this book, I wish you all the luck in the world.

Thank you for reading, Merry Christmas, Happy Birthday, Valentines and anniversary.

Georgia Mae Rose

Bonus Gift Buying Cheat Sheet

- It's not about You
- Think about their highest values
- Solve their problem
- Pitch in together
- Buy one big guaranteed winner or spread the risk with multiple small gifts
- Use their prized possession to your advantage
- Try to understand their values
- Find out what their goals are and see if you can help
- Do you know their dream or vision for the future, can you keep that dream alive?
- Do your research, ask friends and family for ideas, look for interests in their online profile
- Try to replace a lost item if you know of

one.

- Reignite an old interest or passion with a nostalgic gift relating to their past
- Give someone an experience rather than an object or both
- Giving an instant gratification gift is ok but something more fulfilling like a hobby type gift is much better.
- Make the opening experience just as exciting as the gift by being creative
- Give gifts at random times
- Hide gifts in random places for them to discover
- Don't buy a joke present for someone with no sense of humor
- Never regift within the social or family circle
- Be grateful and gracious
- Personalizing gifts can be a great way to honor another person or a special

moment

- Memberships and subscriptions are the gifts that keep on giving
- Needs are more practical but wants are wants
- It's Not About You

www.ingramcontent.com/pod-product-compliance
Lightning Source LLC
Chambersburg PA
CBHW051734290426
43661CB00123B/269